I pray you will see⌁ ⌁⌁⌁ ⌁⌁ ⌁⌁⌁⌁⌁⌁⌁⌁ ⌁⌁⌁⌁ ⌁⌁ His Word and learning to worship at the sink. As women, much time gets spent here; use it wisely. Don't think of the sink as just a place to wash dishes; make it a place of prayer and Scripture memorization. As you read, take those thoughts and verses to the sink and worship as you wash. Let God meet and minister to you as you go through your daily responsibilities.

The sink is often the only place we are left alone with our thoughts, so I want you to intentionally turn your heart to the Lord. It can also be a place where you stand with others, either helping or teaching. May Jesus be seen in you while you're at the sink.

I have written from my heart as a wife and mother. If you are a wife but not a mother, some days may not seem to apply to you yet, and the same goes for being a mother and not a wife. Each day has principles you can apply to your life because we all are teaching someone, even if we don't realize it. For the single mother, your children need to know God's Word and see you setting a godly example in your actions and attitude. Using Scripture as your guide, you can speak to your children about godly marriage during your singleness. Whatever your situation, God has a purpose for you. Look to His Word to learn or be reminded of your influence in your home.

Some of these topics are challenging to write about and even more challenging to receive. I had to receive these from the Lord before ever being able to share them with you. You'll see that I have a straightforward approach, as I believe Scripture does, to the topics. My intention is not to be harsh but to be clear and to help you grasp the gravity of being the godly woman God wants you to be. If we do not take God's Word seriously, we will destroy our homes from the inside (Proverbs 14:1). While I am black-and-white, I also want you to feel like you're sitting at the table talking to a friend who loves you and wants to help you.

In these pages, you will see what the Bible says about your attitude, character, role, and responsibilities as a woman of God. I pray you are challenged and encouraged.

With Hope in His Service,
Heather Helmering

All Scripture is from the King James Version.
Author owns the copyright to all content.

Day One
Godly Homemaking

Godly homemaking depends on a godly woman. You do not have to be a wife, mother, or unemployed to be a homemaker. If you have a home and are a woman, you can and should be a homemaker.

What comes to mind when you think of homemaking? For many, that view is usually extreme. You most likely imagine Little House on the Prairie or Pinterest. Do you envision a lady in a dress and apron hanging laundry out to dry or hand-kneading bread in a perfectly aesthetic kitchen? Most women will not have either of these entirely but fall somewhere in the middle.

Homemaking is "the creation and management of a home, especially as a pleasant place in which to live."

You get to decide if your house will be a home, if you will be a homemaker or just a housekeeper. Scripture gives many qualities of a godly woman and homemaker. This is not an exhaustive list, but an excellent place to start.

1. Wisdom. If you are a wise woman, you will build your home. Proverbs 14:1 says, "Every wise woman buildeth her house: but the foolish plucketh it down with her hands."

You get to choose.

You will not be the wise woman God desires you to be apart from His Word. You must read and study God's

Word and seek Him in prayer. The world, the flesh, and the devil will not lead you to be a godly woman.

2. Pure Speech. Proverbs 15:1-4, 7 says, "A soft answer turneth away wrath: but grievous words stir up anger. The tongue of the wise useth knowledge aright: but the mouth of fools poureth out foolishness. The eyes of the Lord are in every place, beholding the evil and the good. A wholesome tongue is a tree of life: but perverseness therein is a breach in the spirit. The lips of the wise disperse knowledge: but the heart of the foolish doeth not so." Proverbs 16:24 says, "Pleasant words are as an honeycomb, sweet to the soul, and health to the bones." Proverbs 18:21 teaches, "Death and life are in the power of the tongue: and they that as love it shall eat the fruit thereof."

3. Kindness. Proverbs 31:26, "She openeth her mouth with wisdom and in her tongue is the law of kindness." Ephesians 4:32, "And be ye kind one to another, tenderhearted, forgiving one another, even as God for Christ's sake hath forgiven you."

4. Humility. "A man's pride shall bring him low: but honour shall uphold the humble in spirit" (Proverbs 29:23). "Before destruction the heart of man is haughty, and before honour is humility" (Proverbs 18:12).

5. Unselfish. "But this I say, He which soweth sparingly shall reap also sparingly; and he which soweth bountifully shall reap also

bountifully" (2 Corinthians 9:6). "She stretcheth out her hand to the poor; yea, she reacheth forth her hands to the needy" (Proverbs 31:20).

6. God-fearing. "Favour is deceitful, and beauty is vain: but a woman that feareth the LORD, she shall be praised" (Proverbs 31:30).

All of these attributes depend on fearing the Lord. If you do not revere God and His Word, you will not seek to obey His Word. This leaves you doing things your way, usually the opposite of His. Seeking to be a God-fearing woman leads to fulfilling the other attributes, thus making your presence and home a place others want to be. Creating a home, not just a house. It does not matter how well-decorated the house is if your attitude is not inviting.

You do not have to have the newest furniture, perfect meals, or a Pinterest-worthy entryway to have a home where people feel welcome and loved; you just need the presence of the Lord. The goal is godliness, not perfection. If you have a Pinterest-perfect home, that is fine! Just be sure to use it to minister to or encourage others.

Seek God at the sink, and ask Him to help you be a godly homemaker.

Day Two
Virtuous

The next few days will be a study through the attributes of the Proverbs 31 Woman.

"Who can find a virtuous woman? for her price is far above rubies" (Proverbs 31:10).

This is not an attribute only for unmarried ladies. Virtue is often associated with physical purity and saving that for marriage. That is biblical. However, what about once you are married? Being virtuous still applies. Virtue is a lifelong lifestyle.

Flirting, adultery, wearing immodest clothing to catch another man's eye, and sharing marriage problems with another man for sympathy are all examples of not being virtuous. You must maintain your virtue and stay pure to your husband. God puts a high price on virtue.

"The heart of her husband doth safely trust in her, so that he shall have no need of spoil" (Proverbs 31:11).

She is trustworthy. She earned his trust because she was virtuous. Her husband is not worried about her being unfaithful to him. Trust is vital in marriage, as I am sure you know. He trusts her in all areas. He knows she is not a gossip, nor will she bring him any shame. He is glad to be her husband.

The Bible says he has no need of spoil. This word can be applied in two ways: as if something went bad, like milk. He has no fear of his wife spoiling his reputation. If you don't believe your actions impact your husband's reputation, look at 1 Timothy 3.

Secondly, when armies overtook a city, the items they brought back, such as gold, animals, and possessions, were referred to as spoils. This man in Proverbs 31 has no need of anything. He does not lack respect, love, or support. His wife has things in order. She is his helpmeet.

Dear wife, if you were asked this simple question: "Does your husband feel like the most respected and appreciated man in the world?" What would your answer be? What would his answer be?

Apply this to your marriage today. Be a woman your husband can trust completely.

Seek God at the sink and ask Him to seal these truths in your heart and show you any areas that need work.

Day Three
Work Willingly

"She seeketh wool, and flax, and worketh willingly with her hands. She is like the merchants' ships; she bringeth her food from afar. She riseth also while it is yet night, and giveth meat to her household, and a portion to her maidens. She considereth a field, and buyeth it: with the fruit of her hands she planteth a vineyard...She layeth her hands to the spindle, and her hands hold the distaff...She maketh fine linen, and selleth it; and delivereth girdles unto the merchant...She looketh well to the ways of her household, and eateth not the bread of idleness" (Proverbs 31:13-16, 19, 24, 27).

She was not lazy, nor was she a complainer. How powerful! Her entire testimony is given through her actions! The Bible only says she speaks with kindness and wisdom, but never any specific comments or conversations. More about this later.

She sought good ingredients to use to make clothes and food. Wool and flax are for textile uses, and flax can also be used for food. Today, so many ingredients and materials are easily accessible. This verse does not imply that you must make every meal and article of clothing from scratch. You can, and those are excellent skills to have and share, but it does not make you less of a godly woman if you can't or don't do those things.

Just be conscious of what you allow into your and your family's bodies, and learn to make healthy choices. There will be long days or days when you are sick, and picking up a pizza for dinner is more convenient than cooking, but this shouldn't be the usual. Make it a goal to cook good meals for your family and eat at the table together.

She works willingly with her hands. It's one thing to work with your hands and get things done. It is an entirely different thing to work *willingly.* Are you grumbling and complaining the whole time you cook meals, clean your home, or run errands? This is not a willing attitude. Are you a procrastinator? That is also not working willingly. Pray to have the joy of the Lord in everyday tasks.

She brings her food from afar. In those days, much of their merchandise came from other places. She was willing to do what it took to meet her family's needs. Do you find it too troubling to stop at more than one grocery store to get what you need, or get upset when the grocery pickup lacks an item you wanted?

She is up before the sun preparing food for the day. Not because there was anything spiritual about being up before the sun but because she needed to be up early to take care of things for the day. No one in her home is left uncared for. You have to be willing and unselfish to give up sleep. This is so important. Today, there are a lot of wives who make their husbands care for themselves. This is not okay. I understand some things are preferences. Maybe your husband prefers doing his laundry, or perhaps he enjoys cooking. I am not talking about this. I am speaking of *refusal* to care for him because of the attitude of "he's an adult." Of course, he is an adult and capable of doing for himself, but doing things for him should not be viewed as a burden. You are also an adult, but you probably like it when he does things you could do for yourself, such as picking up something on his way home, putting gas in the car, or running an errand.

Grumbling, huffing, and stomping through the house tell your family they are a burden or inconvenience. You should not send this message to those God has given you.

She bought a field and planted a vineyard. If you have ever had a garden, farm, or vineyard, you know this is hard work. She looked for a field that was fit to be used; she had to prepare the ground, plant the seeds, pull the weeds, water it, and when it began to produce, she had to harvest it. Tending a field is no easy task, especially when you have other responsibilities. You do not have to have a garden or vineyard to be a godly woman.

She made their clothes, blankets, and other linen needs, like curtains. Sewing is not a quick task. Not only did she make these things, she had to mend them when they needed it. Plus, she made enough to sell! It is okay to be a stay-at-home mom/wife and still do something for extra income as long as it does not take time away from your other responsibilities. In today's world, many corporations have work-from-home positions, and we have a variety of direct sales companies to choose from. You may even be able to babysit in your home.

Your sewing skills do not determine your spirituality, thankfully! God is seeking willing workers, not professional seamstresses. He wants you to work willingly in your home.

Looking well to the ways of your household and not being idle should be every woman's goal and desire. Rest is needed, vacations are great, and family time is necessary. Don't be so consumed in doing tasks that your family doesn't get time with you. You aren't working our way to godliness. There will be more about idleness later.

You should keep your home clean. It takes a lot of time and energy to keep up a home, especially when you do not live alone, but it is worth the effort. Teach your children to help. Ask your husband for help when you need it. Do not procrastinate and allow it to get so out of hand that it's overwhelming and takes days to get back in order. Mess usually adds to stress levels. Most women do not function well in chaos, and your husband does not feel he can relax in a messy home. A clean home is a happy home.

Seek God at the sink and ask Him to give you the willingness to serve your family and the strength to keep a tidy home.

Day Four
Physically Fit

"She girdeth her loins with strength, and strengtheneth her arms" (Proverbs 31:17).

She had to be physically fit to have the strength and energy to do those things! It can be easy to forget that the people in Scripture were real. Managing the home, children, meals, garden, etc., is hard work, which was no different in those days.

Does this mean you must be a size three and be in the gym five days a week? Not at all. Do you have to buy a blender and have four smoothies made with kale and protein powder daily? Of course not. It means you should be healthy. Learn to make healthy meals and have healthful habits. These are not just for you but for your family, too.

Your body is the dwelling place of the Holy Spirit if you are saved. Do your best to take care of it. Exercise is not only for fanatics and bodybuilders. Eating healthy does not mean you can never have ice cream again. However, you should be conscious and intentional about your health.

You are careful to shower daily, wear clean clothes, brush your teeth, and use deodorant. Eating well is no different. You should want to take care of your body. God did not specify a dress size or weight as "healthy." Everyone is different, with different needs and health situations. Healthy and fit for me may not look the same for you. And that is okay!

Buy a cookbook and try new recipes, get on Pinterest and get new ideas, or ask a friend for tips. You have unlimited access to so many resources! Being healthy has never been easier, but it also has never been more challenging. This is why it takes being intentional and possibly learning new habits.

Overall, people are addicted to sugar and instant gratification. You can pick up processed, artificial food at the grocery store that cooks in the microwave, and every type of restaurant is just around the corner with drive-through, delivery, and curbside pickup options. It's *easier* to pick up pizza, tacos, and donuts than to plan, prepare, and cook a meal. But God does not want you to live a lifestyle of instant gratification. He wants you to be a wise steward of your health.

A dirty kitchen is often the motivator to pick up a meal instead of cooking, isn't it? However, you don't buy new clothes instead of washing what you have, do you? That would be expensive and silly. It is no different when it comes to food.

She brought her food from afar. She prepared food for her entire home. You can model this example. If you are too busy to make a meal plan, grocery shop, and cook a meal, you are too busy. It may be time to evaluate where you spend your time.

Working out is time-consuming. It is not convenient. It is a sacrifice of time and energy. You can do things as a family, such as bike rides, walks and hikes, or swimming. Be creative! The idea is to stay active. Move your body. That's it. It is much more comfortable to stay in pajamas, on the couch, scrolling social media, or binge-watching Netflix than exercise or meal plan.

These habits are hard to break! But you can do it! One day, one meal at a time. Don't beat yourself up for that ice cream cone or for not taking a walk today. Aim to do better tomorrow. Get an accountability partner, ask your spouse to join you, whatever it takes. Starting is the hardest part.

It is important to remember that your health is more than your physical diet. What you feed on mentally, emotionally, and spiritually is just as important as the physical food you fuel your body with. Who you follow on social media, the music and podcasts you listen to, the television shows you watch, and the books you read all must be evaluated against the truths of Scripture.

"I can do all things through Christ which strengtheneth me" (Philippians 4:13).

Seek God at the sink and ask Him to guide you to healthier living.

Day Five
Financially Wise

"She perceiveth that her merchandise is good: her candle goeth not out by night" (Proverbs 31:18).

She had food and clothing for her household, bought a field, and planted a vineyard. She used her resources for good, to care for her family, as every woman should. What that looks like for me may not be the same for you, and that's okay. God desires for your spending to honor Him. Remember that all of your resources and belongings are His. You are just a steward.

James 1:7 says, "Every good gift and every perfect gift is from above, and cometh down from the Father of lights, with whom is no variableness, neither shadow of turning."

"Let a man so account of us, as of the ministers of Christ, and stewards of the mysteries of God. Moreover it is required in stewards, that a man be found faithful" (1 Corinthians 4:1-2). You are a steward of the Gospel, and God expects faithfulness in all areas.

As a wife, you do not have to be in charge of your household finances to be wise with them. Trusting your husband's leadership with finances is hard for some of you. Maybe he isn't financially wise and has put you and your family in a tight place before. I know it's hard, but I firmly believe he has the final authority. You can voice your opinion and have a conversation, but he gets the final say. If he says to pay the internet bill two weeks late, it's just two weeks late. It's not the end of the world.

Please do not sneak around and spend money behind your husband's back. Dishonesty will not honor the Lord or your marriage.

Make your finances and spending a matter of prayer. Nothing is too small for the Lord to be concerned with!

"Casting all your care upon him; for he careth for you" (1 Peter 5:7). All means all!

The Bible has an abundance of Scriptures about how we should conduct ourselves financially. God will give wisdom; just ask.

"If any of you lack wisdom, let him ask of God, that giveth to all men liberally, and upbraideth not; and it shall be given him" (James 1:5).

Seek God at the sink for financial wisdom and help trusting your husband's leading, especially when you disagree.

Day Six
Unselfish

Proverbs 31:20 says, "She stretcheth out her hand to the poor; yea, she reacheth forth her hands to the needy."

As you drive through town, you see the homeless people sitting outside the shelter, the grocery store, and intersections. Are you expected to give to them all? Wouldn't that be a perfect example of being unselfish?

You should give if God leads you to do so. You must listen to the Holy Spirit here. Most people can't afford to give to everyone they see, and there is a level of suspicion if the person truly is in need.

You are to be prepared. You must have food and other supplies to take care of your family. God calls you to be a wise steward. Saving and preparing for the future is not the same as selfishness.

If a missionary comes through, are you quick to give a love offering? Are you willing to bear someone else's burden? To serve when the pastor says there is a need? What about that new family that just moved here? Are you willing to help unload the truck, make a meal, or spend time with them so they feel welcome?

What about being unselfish in your home? Often, this is where things begin to slack. Too many women are more willing to serve those outside than those inside the home. Remember that the Proverbs 31 woman was up before the sun to prepare for the needs of others? As women, society says you need time to recharge because you can't pour from an empty cup, but the truth is that you can, and you do. The Lord has a way of giving you what you need when you rely on Him. That is the type of recharging you need. Rely on Him through joyful obedience when caring for your family. It may be that you don't have the joy of the Lord because you haven't stepped out into this area of obedience yet. Additionally, treat your husband with the same willingness as your children. Do not put him or your marriage at the bottom of your priority list.

It is easy to be selfish with your time and resources. Remember that God may have given *to* you so He can give *through* you. All you have is not yours. You will not run out when you spend God's resources to do God's work. He owns the cattle on a thousand hills and the wealth in every mine. He is your heavenly Father who knows how to give good gifts to His children. He has promised to provide all your needs according to His riches. He will take care of you.

Luke 21 gives the account of the widow and her two mites. First Kings 17 gives the account of Elijah and the widow woman. Over and over again, the provision of God comes when there is obedience to His leading.

Be wise with what God has given you. Obey His leading by giving your time, resources, and energy to further His work.

Seek God at the sink and ask Him to help you to be unselfish with your time, energy, and other resources.

Day Seven
Prepared

Proverbs 31:21-22 says, "She is not afraid of the snow for her household: for all her household are clothed with scarlet. She maketh herself coverings of tapestry; her clothing is silk and purple."

You do not have to know how to sew to be a godly woman, but if you can sew, please offer to teach a younger lady this precious skill.

Do you find yourself struggling with particular needs your family has? Consider a few examples:

1. School starts about the same time every year, yet you wait until the last minute to find clothes and supplies for your children, and when you go to the stores, they are nearly empty- causing you to become frustrated with everyone else for buying all the things you need. Waiting until the last minute to shop is not being prepared.
2. Your family needs dinner every evening, yet choosing not to think about this until 2 P.M. is not being prepared.
3. Christmas, birthdays, and anniversaries come at the same time every year. Rushing out a day or two before, running around like a crazy person trying to find gifts, is not being prepared. Not to mention the stress and the financial burden this adds to you. Not to mention the arguing between you and your spouse because of this.

Break the cycle. Stop doing the same things every year!

She was prepared with clothing for her family before the winter snow came. She didn't wait until the first snow came to run to the market for supplies and had food in their home for everyone. She was prepared.

Just think ahead. This looks different for everyone. If you are married, talk with your spouse about ways to plan and prepare for the future. Make this a matter of prayer, asking the Lord how to prepare better. He cares about all aspects of your life!

A primary way to start is to have a savings account. You don't have to be a financial genius to handle your finances wisely. Do not be afraid to seek counsel from others! God cares about our finances. We just have to trust Him and be obedient to His word. He has given us guidelines and examples to follow.

Seek God at the sink and ask Him to help you prepare for your family's needs.

Day Eight
Honorable

"Strength and honour are her clothing; and she shall rejoice in time to come" (Proverbs 31:25).

Webster's dictionary defines this as "bringing or worthy of honor." It is a synonym for characteristics like morally correct, honest, righteous, virtuous, respectable, etc.

She is clothed with strength and honour. These are what she puts on every day. As you get dressed every morning, you decide what to wear. She chose to put on strength and honor. Something else about clothing is that it's what others see about you first. She didn't behave wickedly and then demand to be called honorable. She *acted* honorable and earned that title. It was a view of her that others had. In 1 Peter 3:3-6, Peter describes how women should be adorned. The Bible says to be meek and quiet, respectable, not only focusing on outward appearance. However, this isn't to say you ignore your outer appearance. She is careful about keeping her testimony, and you should be as well.

Do you know how *hard* it is to be meek and quiet? It's impossible without the help of the Holy Spirit, and even then, you will still blow it sometimes. Please do not ever mistake meekness for weakness. There is GREAT strength in this.

Proverbs 16:32 says, "He that is slow to anger is better than the mighty; and he that ruleth his spirit than he that taketh a city."

She can rejoice and have joy because she is a godly woman. She knows God's way is perfect. Her joy comes from the Lord, as should yours. Being a Christian does not mean life is easy; you know that. It means you can have inner peace and joy through any trial because of Jesus.

Let Him be your joy. Seek God at the sink and ask Him to help you to be a woman after His heart, trusting in Him fully.

Day Nine
Prudent

"She openeth her mouth with wisdom; and in her tongue is the law of kindness" (Proverbs 31:26).

Merriam-Webster defines prudent as having or showing good judgment and restraint, especially in conduct or speech.

The Oxford Languages dictionary defines it as acting with or showing care and thought for the future. You can apply both definitions here.

There are no recorded words from her, but there are things to be learned based on these two characteristics. She does not say things flippantly. She is aware that her words have influence and consequences. She is wise. Her words and actions reflect that, and they align with each other. She does not behave or speak in a way that is contrary to Scripture or harmful to others.

Proverbs 19:14 says, "House and riches are the inheritance of fathers: and a prudent wife is from the LORD."

"Prudent" and "prudence" are often found in Proverbs. God has a lot to say about prudent and foolish persons. All of Proverbs 31 shows that she is prudent, and God desires you to be prudent.

When you open your mouth, is it with wisdom and kindness? Do you find yourself having to apologize for your words often? Do you have frequent times of speaking before you think? Do your words or actions embarrass your husband, causing him to apologize for you? This is not prudence.

Sure, you can apologize for hurtful words, but how much better would it be to speak in wisdom and kindness instead? Pray to have speech that is encouraging, wise, kind, and pleasing to God and others.

What would your home be like if you changed how you spoke to your husband and children? When you speak with wisdom and kindness, you are also building trust. Your husband and kids want to tell you about their day, struggles, and victories because they're not worried about how you will react. Others want to confide in you. Prudence builds friendships and strengthens the body of Christ as a whole.

You want prudent people in your life. People you can go to for help and advice who won't mock you, gossip about you, or belittle you—someone you can trust. You can be that person for yourself, your family, and others.

Seek to have a testimony that pleases God with your words and actions. Think about how your words will affect others. Be quick to hear and slow to speak, as James 1:19 says.

Ask God for help with this as David did. Psalm 141:3 says, "Set a watch, O Lord, before my mouth; keep the door of my lips."
Psalm 19:14 says, "Let the words of my mouth, and the meditation of my heart, be acceptable in thy sight, O Lord, my strength, and my redeemer."

Seek God at the sink and ask Him to help you to be a prudent woman in speech and actions.

Day Ten
Productive & Purposeful

Proverbs 31:27 says, "She looketh well to the ways of her household, and eateth not the bread of idleness."

The first thing that comes to mind is that she probably didn't have many days of thinking that time went by so fast, and she didn't get anything done. Maybe you have read the entire chapter, and you think, "Obviously, she isn't lazy! I read everything she was doing! Who can be idle when they have a husband and children, anyway?"

However, nothing is in God's Word by accident. So, does that mean you *can* be idle despite your responsibilities? Of course, it does.

Looketh well comes from the Hebrew meaning "to lean forward, to peer into the distance." Remember the last verse? She was wise and prudent and looked ahead. That same characteristic is shown here. This time, it's not her words; it's her actions. She looks ahead and sees what results she can expect in the future from today's actions. This prevents procrastination. She knows that being lazy, doing things halfway, and giving her energy to temporal things will not build her home. Proverbs 14:1 says, "Every wise woman buildeth her house: but the foolish plucketh it down with her hands."

Way refers to a walk or step, a way of life. Household, of course, is the family. Remember what your family is—people with souls, needs, and your particular assignment. There is no "just" in God's employment. You are not "just" a wife or mother. Do not diminish what He has called you to do.

Where have you gotten lazy in your home? Maybe you don't keep things as tidy as you once used to. Perhaps you've settled for frozen pizzas and drive-through meals instead of cooking like you once did. Has your phone taken over the time you used to spend doing devotions with your husband or children?

Giving into fleshly desires because it's easy will not build a godly home with children who are spiritually confident and strong. Apathy will not train them to be young men and women who are ready to leave home and start their own families.

Teaching and training the children and caring for your husband and home will take time, effort, energy, and denial of the flesh. But the rewards are priceless. You can be a Proverbs 31 woman. These attributes are not unattainable. God's grace is sufficient to help you become a woman who builds her home.

It is not a sin to rest or make easy meals. God is also a God of balance and rest. He gave that example in Creation when He rested on the seventh day. The Bible records Jesus sleeping and resting as well. Do not think you have to be busy every waking hour of the day to be a godly woman. You are not working your way to godliness. There will be sickness, busy seasons, and unexpected events. You have to adapt to each day and season. Purpose, prudence, and productivity should be characteristics of your life.

Seek God at the sink and pray to be a godly wife and mother who is intentional with her time and energy.

Day Eleven
Idleness

Proverbs 31:27 says, "She looketh well to the ways of her household, and eateth not the bread of idleness."

What comes to mind when you hear the word "idle"? Maybe laziness or sitting still? I used to think of that until the Lord gave me this illustration.

Think of a car. When it idles, what is happening? As that car idles, it's not moving. It is working, though. The engine runs. Inside the engine, the oil moves. Coolant flows. The pistons move and create combustion. Spark plugs ignite, crank and camshafts turn, and sensors monitor all systems. A LOT is going on here. That engine will idle until the car runs out of gas or something breaks. It will work and work, burn lots of gas, but never move the car. If you let it idle enough, wear and tear will eventually occur even though the car never moved. Gasoline engines aren't designed to idle for an endless amount of time.

Does that change your view of being an idle Christian, wife, or mother? When was the last time you said or thought, "I've been so busy all day, but nothing got done!" Or, "Dinner time already?! Where did my day go?"

Now, I will pause here to say a few things. Being a mother and wife is a full-time responsibility. Working outside the home and trying to balance home life is a full-time responsibility. Some days, you do need to rest. Being sick is not part of idleness.

However, you can spend so much time and energy but get nowhere.

Are you so busy you can't make dinner or fold laundry? Do you feel too busy to serve the Lord? Is there time to have devotions and pray? Does this sound like your life? Unfortunately, for most women, it does. Do you often think you could get a handle on things if you just had a few more hours in the day? Friend, more hours are not what you need. You must spend the time that you do have wisely.

Getting started with a new routine is HARD. Being organized and planning ahead takes time and effort. However, it can help you so much. Make realistic goals for each day; don't be afraid to write this in pencil and make changes along the way. You probably create lists for your grocery shopping and what to buy your family for Christmas, but not for your day-to-day tasks. Why is that? Lists keep you focused and on task.

Start today. What would you like done over the next 3-4 days? Don't try to plan a month at a time if it's too much.

I use a monthly view calendar for cleaning and upcoming events. I know cleaning the kitchen and laundry are daily tasks, so I don't write these down, but if you may need to. I have two days when we clean the bathrooms, one day for the floors, one for dusting. I write down that bed sheets need to be changed on Fridays. It's easy to say that I will change the sheets or mop tomorrow…three days in a row. (Don't make that face at me; you've done it, too.) Maybe you struggle with folding the laundry once it's dry. Out of sight, out of mind, right? Rerun the dryer…again to get the wrinkles out.

Maybe you need to schedule a date night with your spouse. It's too easy to say "next weekend" a million times, and that weekend never gets here.

Whatever your needs are, write them down. Write down when your church has activities and outreach so you can attend. If you don't schedule your time, you will continue to sit and wonder where it went. Don't spend it scrolling social media or putting your hard work into things that have no value.

Your time is similar to your finances. Without a budget, money disappears as soon as you get it. Budget your finances and your time so you can spend both effectively.

Seek God at the sink and pray against idleness and wasted time.

Day Twelve
Loveable

Proverbs 31:26, 28-29 says, "She openeth her mouth with wisdom; and in her tongue is the law of kindness. Her children arise up and call her blessed; her husband also, and he praiseth her. Many daughters have done virtuously, but thou excellest them all."

As you read these verses, does she feel like someone you would love? Would you love her company and conversation? Her family calls her blessed. She is kind and caring. She has earned the quality of being blessed and loved by others.

Do you conduct yourself so that those around you love you? Do others love being with you? When you interact with others, are they more encouraged after being around you? Do you seek to build others up instead of tearing them down or being envious of them?

Neglecting this in your home can be easy because you assume your family loves you. You must remember to treat them well, even on the hard days. Do not expect or rely on obligatory love from your family. Always be intentional with your words and actions.

Proverbs 18:24 says, "A man that hath friends must shew himself friendly; and there is a friend that sticketh closer than a brother."

Do not take for granted that you are loved by others, and let your conduct go, assuming their love will remain. While their love may be unconditional, they may not always *like* you.

Ouch.

The Proverbs 31 woman was loveable. She conducted herself in a way that earned love and affection rather than demanding or expecting it. All of the attributes the Bible shares about her explain why she is loveable.

Be careful not to expect others to love you simply because they should, and be careful not to take their love for granted.

Seek God at the sink and ask Him to help you be loveable.

Day Thirteen
God-Fearing

Proverbs 31:30 says, "Favour is deceitful, and beauty is vain: but a woman that feareth the LORD, she shall be praised."

This is not to have a fear in the sense of being scared. Be assured God will not harm you, He loves you unconditionally, and He leads His children in paths of righteousness.

Fear is "A sense of respect, awe, and submission to."

She trusts in God and desires to be right with Him above having favor with others or external beauty. Is this true of you? Favor with others is deceitful because the flesh wants to trust in that. Favor with others can give a sense of security and entitlement. In the workplace, you may say, "I deserved that promotion. We all know that no one even likes Tom."

This is a deceitful favor. What about at church? "Why is she the new nursery director? I've been here longer, and no one even asked me about it." Do not trust in your views rather than the leading of God. You may have been there longer, but that does not mean God has called you to do something over that newer member.

Beauty is vain. Vain means empty. Ladies like to feel pretty and sometimes go to great lengths to make it happen, such as coloring their hair, skin care, makeup, nails, spray tans, botox, and cosmetic surgery. Are these things wrong or sinful? No, you just have to remember that they are empty. They are not eternal, and outer beauty does not earn favor with God. Your inner beauty is what should be the most visible. Do not desire to have favor with others based on your appearance.

Do you fear the Lord? Do you stand in respect and awe at who He is? This view of God should drive you to live a life that serves and honors Him. Her praise comes from what God does in and through her, not in her own works. She was the type of lady that reflected everything back to God. If someone complimented her, she probably said, "Praise the Lord." It's all Him anyway, yet He rarely gets the praise.

Why do you need to fear the Lord?

Proverbs 1:7, "The fear of the Lord is the beginning of knowledge: but fools despise wisdom and instruction." You do not want to be foolish.

Proverbs 10:27, "The fear of the Lord prolongeth days: but the years of the wicked shall be shortened." There are blessings when you fear the Lord.

Psalm 19:9, "The fear of the Lord is clean, enduring for ever: the judgments of the Lord are true and righteous altogether."

Many more verses deal with the fear of the Lord, but I will leave these here and encourage you to search the Scriptures for your own study.

Seek God at the sink and pray for a healthy fear of the Lord.

Day Fourteen
Rewarded

Proverbs 31:31, "Give her the fruit of her hands; and let her own works praise her in the gates."

She did not seek recognition. You know this based on her other qualities. However, the life she lived got the attention of others. She lived for the Lord out loud. A godly lifestyle gains attention from others, both positively and negatively. God calls His children to be separated from the world.

Her family did not praise her falsely. You are known by your fruit/works. Godly living is not an attempt to earn salvation. It is your outward testimony to others. Your words have little effect if you profess Christ with your mouth but not your actions.

While others may praise you for being an encouragement, your faithfulness, or how you serve others, this should ultimately point them back to Jesus. Your life should provoke others to love and good works (Hebrews 10:24). The Proverbs 31 woman's testimony reflected God to the world. It is okay for others to say "Thank you" and "Job well done" when something merits the compliment. It is not wrong to be appreciated. Accepting appreciation or praise is not sinful. Stay humble enough to say "thank you" and "praise the Lord." Give Him the glory.

You should tell people when you are thankful for them and when they have blessed or encouraged you. This is not sinful.

This verse says that the fruit of her own hands and her own works brought the praise. This is not a falsehood. Her family did not praise her for things she didn't do, for being something she wasn't. God is clear that a corrupt tree does not bring forth good fruit (Luke 6:43). Just before this, her husband and children also praised her. These are the ones closest to her. They see who she is day in and day out. You can't hide who you are from these guys, especially toddlers and teenagers. They will call your bluff in a heartbeat! The Proverbs 31 woman is *genuine.*

These characteristics should be found in the life of each Christian lady.

Seek God at the sink and pray to be a woman who lives obediently to His word so you can experience His blessing and draw others to Him.

Day Fifteen
Be a Crown

Proverbs 12:4, "A virtuous woman is a crown to her husband: but she that maketh ashamed is as rottenness in his bones."

The picture this verse paints is lovely. Ask God to give you a renewed appreciation for the beauty of His design, your ministry, and your position as a wife.

Usually, when looking at a crown, you don't think, "That is ugly! Why would someone wear a crown, anyway?"

A crown possesses the image of beauty, value, and prestige. Not everyone walks around with a crown, adding to its value and reservation for significant positions. Even if you have never seen a king or queen, when there is an image on television, social media, or a magazine of someone wearing a crown, they are assumed to be royalty.

A crown is worn on the head, visible for all to see. It is to be displayed and enjoyed. A crown is valuable, and so are you. Even if you do not feel valuable, God says you are, and He has given you the beautiful comparison of being a crown.

As a wife, you should seek to compliment and add beauty and value to your husband. When he introduces you, is he happy to do so, or is he hoping you won't embarrass him? When out in public or fellowshipping with a group, is he on edge about anything you may say or do? When you talk to your friends, is he concerned with how you talk about him?

You should be your husband's biggest cheerleader. One way to do this is never speaking negatively about him to others.

Remember that being virtuous is more than physical purity. It is being morally good, practicing moral duties, and abstaining from vice. Vice is a spot or defect; a fault; blemish. God is not demanding perfection that you cannot obtain. Being virtuous is behaving in a publicly acceptable way, not drawing attention to oneself, and not being in blatant sin.

A crown is simply worn. It does not complain about the wearer, their actions, or choices. It adds its beauty to the wearer, and that's it.

This is not to say you should be seen and not heard, but to remember that the husband is the head and leader of the home *by God's design*. He is the one with that responsibility and burden, not you. It is freeing and exciting when you learn to see that for the blessing it is. You have a beautiful position as a wife.

The opposite is just as absolute and detrimental. She that maketh ashamed is as rottenness in his bones (Proverbs 12:4b). Ouch! Inside your bones is as deep as you can get. Rottenness is a problem that deeply affects everything. Think of someone with bone marrow problems or cancer. It is embedded in their body and takes long, rigorous treatment to fix. It is not surface level. That is what you're doing to your husband if you live in a way that brings shame to him.

Remember, you are one flesh. You are shaming yourself as well as him. Your actions and attitude affect him personally, how others see him, and the ministry he is allowed to have. If you are not a godly woman, he is not allowed to take the office of a deacon. That is a significant burden to bear! Seek to be a crown to your husband and not rottenness in his bones.

I challenge you today to humble yourself in two ways: pray and ask the Lord if anything in your life needs to be changed. Secondly, ask your husband if you do anything that shames or embarrasses him. Definitely pray before the second because it is the hardest of the two.

As challenging as this will be, let this be a good conversation rather than an argument. You won't know if anything bothers him until you ask. Marriage is about becoming more like Christ, growing with your husband, and being one flesh. Choose to complement his life rather than complicate it.

Seek God at the sink and pray to be a crown to your husband so God's design of marriage can be seen through you.

Day Sixteen
Be Like Hur

Exodus 17:8-16 says, "Then came Amalek, and fought with Israel in Rephidim. And Moses said unto Joshua, Choose us out men, and go out, fight with Amalek: to morrow I will stand on the top of the hill with the rod of God in mine hand. So Joshua did as Moses had said to him, and fought with Amalek: and Moses, Aaron, and Hur went up to the top of the hill. And it came to pass, when Moses held up his hand, that Israel prevailed: and when he let down his hand, Amalek prevailed. But Moses' hands were heavy; and they took a stone, and put it under him, and he sat thereon; and Aaron and Hur stayed up his hands, the one on the one side, and the other on the other side; and his hands were steady until the going down of the sun. And Joshua discomfited Amalek and his people with the edge of the sword. And the Lord said unto Moses, Write this for a memorial in a book, and rehearse it in the ears of Joshua: for I will utterly put out the remembrance of Amalek from under heaven. And Moses built an altar, and called the name of it Jehovah–nissi: For he said, Because the Lord hath sworn that the Lord will have war with Amalek from generation to generation."

Hur is a man who is not well known. There are just a few verses about him, many of which are part of genealogy.

Here is the Israelites' first battle on their way into the Promised Land, and Hur is found holding up one of Moses' hands during the battle. Moses was the leader of the Israelites at this time. Look closely at verse 9. Moses says he will go to the top of the hill. Verse 10 shows Aaron and Hur standing by him. It does not appear that Moses *asked* them to go. Aaron and Hur willingly support their leader, the man of God.

In context, this is often preached and taught to remind the church to support the pastor as long as he follows God. To which I agree 110%. However, the attitude and example of Hur can be applied to wives. This kind of servant's attitude and support is needed in homes today.

Hur climbed to the top of the hill with Moses. Do you ever feel like life is an uphill battle? Maybe there are mountain-like trials in your marriage you can't seem to conquer. Be like Hur. Keep climbing. Keep supporting your husband.

Hur jumped into action to help Moses without being asked. He had a servant's heart. Do you? As a wife, you are your husband's help-meet. No one else has that position–just you. Are you there when trials come, when he struggles, needs prayer or encouragement? Or do you have a "that's not my job/problem" attitude? You are one flesh. His problems are yours, too.

The Israelites would have lost the battle if Hur had had that attitude. People would have died, and they would not have gained the land. Something was at stake for them; the same is true for you and your marriage today.

The Israelites had victory because Hur chose to support their leader. Are you supporting the leader God has given you?

Hur supported Moses until the going down of the sun. They were there all day until the battle was over. When your husband, marriage, or family are in the battle, are you there to support him? Hur and Aaron didn't know how long the battle would last. They didn't ask. They just went and supported Moses' hands as long as was needed.

Stay the course. Keep supporting, encouraging, and praying until the battle is over.

Hur was not extensively recognized, publicly thanked, or in a leadership position. He wasn't the leader, nor was he bitter about being in submission to the leadership. Bitterness will not lead you to support your husband.

Likewise, as a wife, you are to submit to your husband's leadership. Not because he is perfect or deserving. But because the Lord said to. The Lord put you two together because you need each other. Maybe your husband will face a battle that needs your prayers and support to win. His battles aren't always about you, or his lack of love, care, and concern for you. Instead of taking it personally, take it to the Lord and pray for your husband.

Choose not to be bitter or hostile but to willingly serve, even if you don't get a "thank you."

Being like Hur means you are invaluable, involved, sometimes invisible, but always an investor.

The Bible is not saying you should be invisible to your husband. He should love and appreciate you. But to the world, the church, and sometimes even your family, your support and sacrifices will be unnoticed or even belittled.

God sees and knows, and your eternal reward awaits you in Heaven. You have to trust that God's way works.

Serve, support, submit, and sacrifice as unto the Lord. So others may see Him through you, not for the recognition and to be told by others that you are such a good wife. Your reward and praise come from God.

Dear wife, your husband needs your support, prayers, encouragement, submission, and sacrifice. You are invaluable to him, others, and your marriage/home. You must be involved to support. If you're watching TV, on your phone, or out with friends all the time, you cannot be involved in your husband's life or your home.

Are you asking him how he is, how his day went, what he needs from you, or how you can pray for him? Those are simple ways to be intentionally involved. If you don't know how to support, just ask!

When you serve like Hur, you invest in your husband, children, and marriage. The result is always eternal rewards. This investment is always worth whatever sacrifices you make to do it.

Do not live this life seeking to get your own way. Seek God at the sink and ask Him how to support your husband and children.

Day Seventeen
Where Did You Hear That?

Have you ever heard your child say something, and you responded, "Where did you hear that?"

Usually, this comes after they say something they shouldn't. Maybe it was a surprise plan they figured out, something they said about another person, or a not-so-nice word they picked up.

Children do not have to be taught to have a bad attitude, complain, argue, or lie. Their sinful nature took care of that, and then their parents spend eighteen years trying to teach them not to speak, think, and act sinfully. Fighting the flesh is a challenging, never-ending battle. And if adults were honest, they still battle these things.

Do you remember the Israelites in the Old Testament? Numbers 21:5 says, "And the people spake against God, and against Moses, Wherefore have ye brought us up out of Egypt to die in the wilderness? for there is no bread, neither is there any water; and our soul loatheth this light bread."

These are the children and grandchildren of the adults Moses led out of Egypt nearly 40 years before this. Some of them weren't even alive, and they were asking why Moses led them around the wilderness. They were born in this wilderness! It's all they have known! It sounds like they are just repeating what they've heard, doesn't it?

They listened to their parents and grandparents complain. They heard them say things were better in Egypt. Why wouldn't they question God and Moses after hearing this so often? They are doubting God based on their parents' opinions. This is why our attitude and speech are so important! Our kids listen and form their opinion of God based on our example!

Numbers 14:2-3 says, "And all the children of Israel murmured against Moses and against Aaron: and the whole congregation said unto them, Would God that we had died in the land of Egypt! or would God we had died in this wilderness! And wherefore hath the LORD brought us unto this land, to fall by the sword, that our wives and our children should be a prey? were it not better for us to return into Egypt?"

They were so upset, looking at their circumstances rather than God, that they wanted to return to Egypt! Back to slavery!

Now, don't be too hard on them. Have you ever thought about quitting on God–not serving, not going to church anymore, leaving where God has you for something that seems better? Most people have had these thoughts at least once. Even Peter returned to fishing after the crucifixion.

During times of struggle, worry, and doubt, learn to focus on your Saviour rather than your circumstances. How you handle difficult situations will either encourage your family or discourage them. They need to see you praising and trusting God, not looking to return to Egypt. God has promised in Philippians 4 that when you are living for Him, trying to do right, He will provide all your needs. He is to be your sufficiency. You must learn to trust Him. That promise is conditional, but it is one you can count on.

What are those around you hearing from you? Are you praising the Lord? Are you trusting Him? This is part of why you are to begin your prayer time with a time of praise. Look back on how God has blessed and provided in the past, thank Him for it, be encouraged by it, and keep trusting Him.

Seek God at the sink and ask Him to help you trust and praise Him with your words.

Day Eighteen
Be Ye Angry and Sin Not

"Be ye angry, and sin not: let not the sun go down upon your wrath:" (Ephesians 4:26).

This verse is not condemning anger. Anger is an emotion God gives, but just like all other emotions, it has a place. You are not to live solely based on emotions. Often, strong emotions rise out of either fear or pride.

Anger is one of them. Anger comes when you fear someone hurting your reputation, gossiping about you, ruining relationships, etc. Anger comes when pride rears up and says you "deserve better" than what is happening.

Pride also causes you to take offenses personally. The sins of your friends, family, neighbors, and children are sins against the Lord first and foremost, and you should be righteously angry over sin that breaks God's heart. Sin committed against you genuinely hurts. I am not trying to diminish that at all. But God is the Ultimate Healer, and you must learn to take those wounds to Him rather than holding onto them and being angry at another person.

Your anger does not accomplish anything. It causes physical, emotional, and spiritual issues while not affecting the other person.

You are allowed to be and feel that anger; you just aren't to live there. Anger that is not dealt with turns to bitterness. Bitterness is highly destructive. It creeps into your relationships, even with those who did not hurt you. Bitterness becomes who you are. God calls His children to be joyful and thankful, not bitter.

When you get angry, you often aren't thinking clearly. You get overrun by emotions, fear, and pride. It is as if your brain short-circuits. You do not think of the consequences of your actions. Instead, you act on impulse.

Some people act physically. They become violent, hurting things or other people. They are explosive. This person is sinning in their anger. That is easy to see and agree upon.

Others act verbally. Remember that verbal wounds hurt just as much as physical ones. This person yells, screams, curses, and insults those around them or what caused the anger. Even if the verbal anger is not directed at a person, everyone around the anger feels its effects, and no one feels comfortable. This person is also sinning in their anger.

Let's get down to applying this.

I want to focus on the verbal aspect. Most people agree that controlling your tongue can be challenging and something everyone could do better with. There are things you have always heard from your parents or others, and it is just part of your inner dialogue.

Repeating hurtful or sarcastic things makes them naturally come out of your mouth. Do you even notice them anymore?

How often do you tell your husband or children to "shut up"? How often do you say condescending things such as:

"Can't you do anything right?"

"Are you stupid?"

"You will never be good at anything."

"Is this the best you can do?"

"Why are you so lazy?"

You get the picture. Talking this way is hurtful, unnecessary, and absolutely not pleasing to the Father. It is easy to read those examples and see how mean they are. However, it is different to actually control your words and stop saying them to those you are supposed to love.

These words and phrases are not loving at all. They are destructive. Does your husband speak harshly to you over small mistakes? Make sure you are not also speaking harshly over his small mistakes.

I know someone will point out abusive and narcissistic men here. That is not what is being referred to. Yes, those men exist, and that is sinful behavior. Men are usually credited with anger problems; some men are just this way, regardless of how kind the wife is. I know that. I am not saying your speech is the reason for their hateful words; just be sure it isn't. You are individually responsible to the Lord for your thoughts, words, and actions.

What I am saying is don't be mad at him for being hurtful to you if you are constantly being hurtful to him. Be the one to break the vicious cycle. Choose to be the one to use kind words first.

The same goes for your children. Kids can be mean; they struggle to control their flesh, and they act impulsively.

Teaching them to be kind is a constant process. You may feel like a failure as a parent. The Bible says, "Foolishness is bound in the heart of a child; but the rod of correction shall drive it far from him" (Proverbs 22:15). No parent or child is perfect. But you must listen to the tone and words you speak to them. Sometimes, what you hear from them is just a reflection of what they hear from you.

Your husband and children are gifts from God that He can rightfully take back at any time. Do not mistreat the gifts you have been given. Those are His children you are speaking to, and I assure you that God cares about how you treat His kids. You must stop letting your anger and frustration rule your tongue.

You cannot overcome this alone. You will need the Holy Spirit and the Word of God. He is the only one who can change you. Memorize verses about anger and the tongue, post them around your home, and pray for God's help. He wants to help you. He wants your words to be life-giving, not life-taking.

Proverbs 14:1 says, "Every wise woman buildeth her house: but the foolish plucketh it down with her hands." Do not be a foolish woman. Choose to build your home.

Proverbs 15:1-4 says, "A soft answer turneth away wrath: but grievous words stir up anger. The tongue of the wise useth knowledge aright: but the mouth of fools poureth out foolishness. The eyes of the LORD are in every place, beholding the evil and the good. A wholesome tongue is a tree of life: but perverseness therein is a breach in the spirit." Your words have the power to breach or break someone's spirit.

Proverbs 31:26 says, "She openeth her mouth with wisdom; and in her tongue is the law of kindness." This is an example, not a hopeful suggestion.

Friend, you are not alone in this struggle. So many women battle this. So many know their words and tones are not godly, but they don't know how to break the habit. I was there. God is still growing me in this area.

No wonder God teaches in Titus 2 that the aged women are to teach the younger women how to love their husbands and children! That verse talks of phileo love. You must have kindness, friendship, and brotherly love for your husband. Teach and encourage each other women to do this because it does not always come naturally.

This is not to say never to discipline, correct, use a firm tone, etc. Please understand that. Speaking sarcastically and hatefully should not be a characteristic of the life of a Christian. There will be days that you don't get it right. Apologize to your children and husband when that happens, and of course, always go to the Lord and ask for His forgiveness and help.

Additionally, do not be offended when a friend or older lady points out something you need to work on in this area. She is not doing it to embarrass you. She is doing it to help you. Chances are, she has made the same mistakes and knows the damage that can be done. Be thankful God has given you a lady like that in your life.

Seek God at the sink and ask Him to help you not sin in your anger.

Day Nineteen
Four Keys to Being a Godly Wife

Scripture gives many commands and boundaries for being a godly woman and wife. Here are four keys you can begin to implement today. This is not an all-inclusive list, but it will make a difference and get you to a place of allowing God to work in your life and marriage.

God never intended His Word to be inapplicable or unachievable. His Word is meant to help right where you are. These keys are to encourage you and open the door to growing closer to God and your husband. Apply these daily, and see what God will do in your life and marriage.

1. Be filled with the Holy Spirit. Ephesians 5:18.

You must first be saved. If you are not a Christian, a born-again child of God, then you do not have the Holy Spirit living inside of you. Once you accept Jesus as your Saviour, the Holy Spirit immediately comes to live inside your heart. You need Him to be the wife God wants you to be. The Holy Spirit is the One that helps you to pray, understand Scripture, and do or stop doing something so that you live and act according to Scripture. You need His prompting and leading!

2. Change your thinking. 1 Corinthians 10:31 and Ephesians 6:6.

You are serving the Lord through your marriage just as much as serving Him in the choir, nursery, or teaching a Sunday School class. Your marriage is a ministry and should be done as unto and for the Lord Jesus Christ. With joy, love, and a willing heart.

3. Pray, pray, pray. 1 Thessalonians 5:17, James 5, Matthew 26:41.

You must be a woman of prayer. You must be seeking God daily for strength and wisdom. Prayer is how we learn more about God, how He changes you, and how He may even change your husband. Taking the time to pray is vital. So many blessings are missed due to a lack of prayer. God did not speak so much about prayer for us to disregard it or treat it as optional. Your prayer life is lacking if you are not praying for your husband.

4. Fast. Matthew 17:21. Jesus taught about fasting while He was on Earth. Scripture shows the importance of it and how some things you face will require prayer and fasting. Fasting leads you deeper with the Lord. It brings a new level of dependence on Him; in times of trial, depending on God is what you need. Fasting can be done privately, or you and your husband can fast together. Just follow the Lord's leading. Fasting may also be required when your husband faces a decision or spiritual battle. Sometimes, God leads you to fast on behalf of others. Be thankful for

the opportunity to intercede on your husband's behalf, even if you do not enjoy fasting or know why God is asking you to do it.

Use these keys to grow closer to the Lord and your husband.

Seek God at the sink and ask Him to grow you into a godly wife and the wife your husband needs.

Day Twenty
Walking in Love

Ephesians 5:1-2 says, "Be ye therefore followers of God as dear children; And walk in love, as Christ also hath loved us, and hath given himself for us an offering and a sacrifice to God for a sweetsmelling savour."

This may be a very familiar passage to you. It is easy to get acquainted with Scripture and gloss over things rather than truly study them. Ephesians chapters 1-3 talk about the riches in Christ Christians have access to through salvation. Chapters 4-5 get to practical application by telling us how to walk and live out our faith. Chapter 6 deals with the reality of spiritual warfare and how to prepare for it. Chapter 5 deals with the family unit later on, and remembering the placement of that passage is essential.

After God has said who you are and what you have in Christ, verse 1 starts with "therefore." This is saying, "Because of everything we just talked about, now this is what you are to do." This is how God wants you to live.

He says Christians are to be followers of God as dear children. Following Him means you are to imitate Him.

Next, He says you are to walk in love. Walking is a repeated motion. You are to repeatedly behave in a way that displays love. Love is an action word, not just a bunch of warm fuzzy feelings. You can choose to love someone even if you don't have feelings. First Corinthians 13 also gives many characteristics of what biblical love is. Here, God says to mimic Him in the way you love.

Christ gave himself for you. Calvary was God's display to the world of His love for humankind. I would like to apply this to your marriage, even though God applies this to your life as a whole, so this is still in context.

Notice the way Christ loves you. He gave Himself willingly and sacrificially. He didn't hold anything back. He did this for you, for everyone. There is a need that you could not meet on your own. He saw that need. He met that need before you asked Him to. He gave Himself for all, knowing many will never accept what He did. He died for you without asking you to earn it or pay Him back. Is this the way you love your husband? Do you go out of your way for him? Do you meet his needs without him asking? Do you do it willingly? Willingness and sacrifice are part of Christ-like love.

If you only halfway meet a need your spouse has, refuse to be helpful, or keep score of what they've done for you or how they've treated you, you are not loving. This is not servanthood; this is being a willing, loving helpmeet.

Many wives miss out on the joy and blessings God has when they choose not to be kind and loving to their husbands. Love is not selfish. Christ is not selfish. Love does not seek its own. Rather than saying things like, "I don't have to," "That's not my job/problem," or "They're an adult and can do it themselves," why don't you try going out of your way and doing something for him just because you love him?

You are an adult, but I assume you still prefer your husband to take you out to eat, even though you know how to cook. You like him to wash your car, maintain it, or put gas in it, even though you should know how to do it yourself. Most women want to be taken care of, spoiled, etc., but do not give their husbands the same treatment. Do you really think he doesn't need or deserve to be cared for? Do not treat your husband as a burden or afterthought and then get mad because he isn't spoiling you or get frustrated because you don't have the blessings of God in your marriage. Why would He bless you when you are living contrary to His Word?

Be humble enough to get on your knees before God and ask what you need to change rather than just asking Him to change your husband.

Love is sacrificial, not always convenient, and selfless. Choose to love like Christ and trust Him with the rest.

Proverbs 31:12, "She will do him good and not evil all the days of her life. 31:26, "She openeth her mouth with wisdom; and in her tongue is the law of kindness."

Seek God from the sink and ask Him to help you walk in love.

Day Twenty-One
Will You Let Him?

The world has taught women that submission to their husbands means you lose who you are. Biblically, that is not true. Submission is just saying yes to God by saying yes to your husband and letting him have the final say. It allows him to walk out the authority and responsibility God has given him. It is freeing for the wife. You get to say, "Okay, Lord. This is the decision my husband made. Please help me to support it, and even though I may disagree, I am asking you to work out the details and help me to trust You."

Most women want their husbands to be strong, steady, and sacrificial. Wives are told their husbands should be strong physically so they can protect and provide, strong spiritually so they can lead and teach, strong emotionally to balance out their emotions and make decisions based on facts, and strong mentally to deal with the pressures of life. They want him to be steady and consistent, to hold a job, not change his convictions or preferences often, and not live by emotions. Men are expected to be sacrificial with their time, resources, and love. Why? Because wives need and want security.

God wired you to desire and need this from your husband. It's not a bad thing! However, your approach may need some work.

Do you want your husband to lead spiritually but negatively respond when he says the family will be at Saturday soul-winning, every night of the missions conference, or family devotions after dinner? Do you roll your eyes, huff, or say no? That's not letting him lead.

Do you want your husband to be strong but get upset when he doesn't easily show or discuss his emotions? To him, strength is keeping his emotions under control.

Do you want him to love sacrificially but make it hard for him, then act like he is the problem?

Do you want him to work steadily and sacrificially, yet you aren't grateful for that sacrifice, making him feel like a paycheck rather than a provider? Do you complain he works too much rather than thanking him for the overtime?

Do you expect perfection, unconditional love, and grace? Do you expect him to go above and beyond for you without question or complaint? Then, meet him with criticism or never thank him? To your husband, not being appreciated feels like a lack of respect and maybe even love.

Being treated this way does not motivate him to do things for or with you, just as you would not be motivated to do something for him if he treated you this way. Your husband needs your support and appreciation. The next time he says he likes things a certain way, a movie or television show is inappropriate, the kids need a set bedtime, etc., support him. He will stop leading if you don't support and encourage his leadership.

I'm not saying it's right. He is still responsible to the Lord for how he leads your family. But God also created you to be his helpmeet. God has given wives a great responsibility and opportunity to support and encourage their husbands. You know what the Bible says they should do, but remember what It says you should also do.

You won't agree with everything he does, and that's okay. Take that to God in prayer and then to your husband privately.

It is easy to say you want him to be strong, steady, and sacrificial, but do you let him be the man you want and the man God calls him to be?

Seek God at the sink. Ask Him to show you the godly qualities of your husband and for wisdom to support and encourage his leading.

Day Twenty-Two
Are You Salty?

Matthew 5:13 says, "Ye are the salt of the earth: but if the salt have lost his savour, wherewith shall it be salted? it is thenceforth good for nothing, but to be cast out, and to be trodden under foot of men."

This verse is part of the Sermon on the Mount that Jesus preached to His disciples, but it is also for you today.

First, Jesus says you are the salt of the earth. "Are" is a present-tense verb. This is part of your identity if you are saved. He did not say to try to be the salt. He said you are the salt. This is not something you decide to be or not to be.

So, what does salt do?

1.   Salt Preserves. It protects from decay. Is this your testimony? Are you protecting and preventing decay in those you are around? As the salt of the earth, you should point others to Jesus. If you are joining in on the gossip, slander, making fun of others, dirty jokes, negativity, or supporting sin, then you are not being salty. That is the salt that has lost its savour.

As a godly woman, you must also be the salt of our home. It is up to you to model a genuinely biblical life in front of your children. You preserve and protect your home by praying for protection over your home, marriage, and children. Satan wants to destroy your life. Prayer is your first line of defense!

Also, your words and actions should not bring decay to others. Proverbs 12:4 says, "A virtuous woman is a crown to her husband: but she that maketh ashamed is as rottenness in his bones." A wife has the power to drain the life out of her husband. Proverbs 14:1 says, "Every wise woman buildeth her house: but the foolish plucketh it down with her hands." A wife also has the power to build or destroy her home. Be sure you are the preserving salt God has called you to be.

2. Salt Seasons.

Just as salt adds flavor and enhances existing flavor, you should be doing the same.

You should add Jesus wherever you go and bring out Jesus even more in the places where He already exists. This brings those who don't know Jesus to Him and encourages those who know Him to keep trusting and living for Him. This world is exhausting; sometimes, other Christians need their faith encouraged. Colossians 4:6 gives a command: "Let your speech be always with grace, seasoned with salt, that ye may know how ye ought to answer every man."

3. Salt Causes Thirst.

Your life should make others want the Living Water inside of you! For salt to have the most significant effectiveness, it must be pure. In Matthew 5:13, the salt was cast out into the dirt. It wasn't useful at all. It was mixed with the earth. No one wants dirt on their food. The same is true for you. When you get mixed up with the world's dirt, you aren't salty anymore. No one cares what a Christian says when they look like the world. You must keep your saltiness to have an impact on those around you.

For others to see Jesus in you, you must be careful with your words, actions, and reactions. How do you speak? Are you cursing, lying, gossiping, or complaining? What about your actions? Where do you go? What do you watch, read, and listen to? Are you selfish? Prideful? Negative? Hateful? Angry? Bitter? How do you react in challenging circumstances or when you are offended?

The world is watching.

When Christians speak, act, and react like the world, they have lost their savour, and the world isn't thirsty for what Christians claim they have. Your words, actions, and reactions must preserve, season, and cause others to thirst. You must reflect Christ.

As a godly woman, this is vital to your home. Your children need you to live like Christ. The world, the flesh, and the devil will tell them they don't need to. You must preserve our homes through prayer and live a godly life that makes them thirst for the Saviour. If you are a wife and mother, be the prayer warrior of your home.

Be the salt.

Seek God at the sink and ask Him to help you live a genuine, godly life.

Day Twenty-Three
Arise and Build

What is God asking you to build as a Christian, wife, and mother?

Your faith?

Your home?

Your testimony?

The heritage you are leaving for your children and grandchildren?

Now, more than ever, women are under attack. Femininity and your place in the home are mocked and belittled. It is time to arise and build.

As a wife, God calls you to build and keep your home. It is time to rise to the call and build.

Your place as a wife and mother is highly valued, which is why Satan is attacking.

Titus 2:5 calls you to be the keeper of the home. Proverbs 14:1 calls you to build your home.

But, I would like to focus on Nehemiah.

Just as Nehemiah saw the city's condition and knew it needed to be rebuilt, I want you to see the needs of your home, marriage, and children. See the need to arise and build.

The first thing Nehemiah did was fast and pray (Nehemiah 1:4). This should be something every Christian does. Prayer and fasting should not be foreign practices! Your spiritual life and that of others depend on your prayer and fasting. These are not outdated practices.

Next, in verse 5, he begins to pray and confess sin. He acknowledged God's power, character, and past doings. This is how you must arise and build. You have to trust the Lord. Obey as He leads.

In chapter 2, in the middle of verse 12, "…what my God had put in my heart to do…"
This was the call of God. As a wife and mother, that is the call of God on your life. He did not give you a family by accident. It is His will for you.

The end of verse 18 says, "…And they said, Let us rise up and build. So they strengthened their hands for this good work." It is time to strengthen your hands. Look to the Lord and purpose to build your home as He wants you to.

Verse 20a says, "Then answered I them, and said unto them, The God of heaven, he will prosper us; therefore we his servants will arise and build:…" You must trust that God will lead, help, and bless when you say yes to doing things His way. It is time to arise and build.

Chapter 3 shows that many people got involved in building the city- the high priest, goldsmiths, regular men, rulers, women, and others.

There are people around you that are willing to help you. Your pastor preaches, Sunday school teachers teach, friends pray and offer counsel, and others that God has given you. Nehemiah could not have rebuilt the city alone. The task was too large. But God also called those other people to get involved. God has called others to get involved in your life, and He has called you to be involved in the lives of others. It may be a minor or temporary involvement, but it is what God wants. Titus 2 is clear that you are to teach others and be teachable.

Chapter 4 shows the attacks of the enemies. You have enemies, too: the world, the flesh, and the devil. You are constantly battling something, whether laziness or apathy, the attack of society, or spiritual warfare. God has laid out what the enemies are, and He has said how to fight them.

Verse 9 says, "Nevertheless we made our prayer unto our God, and set a watch against them day and night, because of them." Prayer is not a one-time thing. You need a steady prayer life.

Verse 17 says they worked with one hand and held a weapon in the other. This is how you must build! The enemy is here, and you must have your weapon ready! Your weapon is the Word of God. As you arise and build, you must also be armed for battle.

There will be days when the battle is raging, and you are weary. You must go to the Word. There will be days when you do not want to build or battle. You must go to the Word. This is not for the weary. Satan is relentless. Your flesh is selfish. But still, you are called to arise and build. You must rely on the Word.

Chapter 6, verse 15 begins with, "So the wall was finished…" One day you will finish your work. But until then, know that you can continue regardless of the fear and opposition you will face. Keep rising. Keep building. Keep trusting God.

Chapter 9 records repenting and confessing sin, which is also not a one-time thing. Keep a short account with God. Verse 3 says they read the book of the law of the LORD, confessed, and worshipped. You must do the same as you build your home for the Lord. You can live this way because He is ready to pardon, gracious, merciful, slow to anger, and of great kindness (verse 17).

God loves you right where you are. Maybe you haven't begun to build your life as He wants you to. Start today.

Perhaps you have gotten away from Him, and the walls you once had are broken down. It's time to repair the wall.

Walls are for safety. They protect those inside from the dangers lurking outside. When there is no wall, you are susceptible to everything. This is not how God wants you to live. He wants you to be protected. The Lord wants you to have convictions and standards. He wants you to say no to sin, no to the world's ways, and yes to Him. God wants you to use the Word as your guide. He wants you to trust Him.

Arise and build.

Chapter 10, verse 39 ends with this phrase, "...and we will not forsake the house of our God." Will you say the same?

Seek God at the sink, and ask Him to guide you as you arise and boldly build your home for Him.

Day Twenty-Four
Parenting in Proverbs

Chapters 2-5 and 7 begins with a plea from a father to his son to listen to the instruction and wisdom. God has not written these chapters for you to ignore them. In these chapters, there is a call to obedience. The plea is given because, in the flesh, you do not naturally listen to godly wisdom; you prefer your own understanding. God clearly states that your way results in sin, destruction, and death (Proverbs 3:5-6 and 14:12).

As a parent, you are responsible for teaching and training your children. They are responsible for obedience, but you are called to teach and model obedience. Children must be expected to obey; if they choose not to, you are to deliver consequences.

God does the same with His children. The law of sowing and reaping applies to everyone, including your children. From toddlers to teenagers, you have a responsibility to your children. The actions and consequences change as they grow but do not disappear. The responsibility of parents to model a godly life never changes regardless of their children's ages.

As a child of God, you are never exempt from God's boundaries. Your children need to know that they'll never outgrow God. You must show them a surrendered life that joyfully seeks God's will and submits to it. If you live apart from God, your children will think they do not need to submit to God's authority once they are adults, leaving them with a life of sin and heartache. Continue to model a surrendered life in front of them.

Secondly, as a wife and mother, you have a responsibility to model godly womanhood to your children. Please do not dismiss the importance of this if you only have sons. Your boys need to see what a godly woman is to determine when a young lady is a potential spouse. They must see these godly qualities lived out.

As a wife, do you willingly submit to your husband's authority in the home? If you don't, your children probably don't either, yet you discipline them for it. They should obey Dad, but you should model this, too. They need to see healthy, biblical communication and obedience. If you are arguing and complaining, they will, too. It starts with you.

As a mom, do you use Scripture to discipline but not encourage? They will feel that God's Word is only a list of rules and God is an angry dictator. This is not the God of the Bible. They must know God's Word encourages and comforts them just as it corrects them.

As a mom, do you point out ways you are obeying Scripture in your life and home? When Dad makes a decision, encourage him to point out Scripture to back it up when possible. When you say a cartoon, show, music, book, etc., is inappropriate, use Scripture. They need to see practical ways to apply God's Word. Not out of pride to say you are better than others or only make good choices, but to show them that God's Word is applicable and that obeying God's Word does not mean life is boring.

Do you share (when appropriate) that you have disobeyed the Lord and need to repent? Maybe it was an argument with your husband, a harsh tone to a child, a word of gossip, a complaining spirit, envy, pride, anger, or laziness. It is okay to tell your children you battle sin and must repent. When you sin against them, apologize and ask for forgiveness. Let them know you recognized the sin, asked the Lord to forgive and help you, and now you ask for their forgiveness, too.

This is something most adults need to improve at. It hurts your pride, but if you do not get ahold of this, a few things will result:

1. Your children struggle with sin and never get help because they think they are the only ones struggling. Satan uses isolation. Let them know you still fight the flesh. Do not leave them struggling alone.
2. They do not learn to apologize and ask for forgiveness. This behavior leaves the world, flesh, and devil in charge, resulting in a narcissist who blames their actions on others rather than taking responsibility for themselves. You must teach and train your children in this area! They need to know how to go to God's Word for help, pray for forgiveness and victory, and get right with one another.

Next, you must teach them to have their own walk with God. Again, this begins with modeling it. They need to see you spending time in your Bible and prayer. They must know that you believe, trust, and rely on God.

Lastly, they need to see you living out the truths of Scripture. They need to see you living out your faith. They need to know the Bible works. If you do not believe it and live it out as much as possible, they won't either. Your children need to see your faithfulness. God needs to be real to them, but it starts with God being real for you.

Seek God at the sink and ask Him to help you parent your children in a way that draws them to Him.

Day Twenty-Five
Truths About Nagging

To Nag is to annoy or irritate (a person) with persistent fault-finding or continuous urging.

Nagging comes easily.

Nagging isn't biblical.

The Reason for Nagging: To get someone to do something you want.

If nagging is not biblical, that means to nag is to sin. Do not justify it by saying that it works.

Synonyms: badger, annoy, berate, harass, bother, irritate, pester, scold.

Antonyms: praise, aid, assist, compliment, delight, encourage, please, make happy.

What a stark contrast!

What the Bible Says About Nagging:

"A continual dropping in a very rainy day and a contentious woman are alike" (Proverbs 27:15).

"A foolish son is the calamity of his father: and the contentions of a wife are a continual dropping" (Proverbs 19:13).

"It is better to dwell in the wilderness, than with a contentious and an angry woman" (Proverbs 21:19).

"It is better to dwell in the corner of the housetop, than with a brawling woman and in a wide house" (Proverbs 25:24).

"Continual dropping" gives the idea of when there's a leaky roof or faucet and the "drip….drip….drip….drip," nearly drives you crazy.

You'll do just about anything to make that sound stop. THAT is the comparison God gives to describe a contentious and nagging wife! I hope you're not purposefully speaking to your husband to annoy him. God calls you to provoke one another to love and good works, not to anger, annoyance, frustration, or housework.

What the Bible Says: The Woman You Should Be.

"A virtuous woman is a crown to her husband: but she that maketh ashamed is as rottenness in his bones" (Proverbs 12:4).

"The heart of her husband doth safely trust in her, so that he shall have no need of spoil. She will do him good and not evil all the days of her life. She openeth her mouth with wisdom; and in her tongue is the law of kindness. She looketh well to the ways of her household, and eateth not the bread of idleness. Her children arise up, and call her blessed; her husband also, and he praiseth her" (Proverbs 31:11-12, 26-28).

"The aged women likewise, that they be in behaviour as becometh holiness, not false accusers, not given to much wine, teachers of good things; That they may teach the young women to be sober, to love their husbands, to love their children, To be discreet, chaste, keepers at home, good, obedient to their own husbands, that the word of God be not blasphemed" (Titus 2:3-5).

"Likewise, ye wives, be in subjection to your own husbands; that, if any obey not the word, they also may without the word be won by the conversation of the wives; Whose adorning let it not be that outward adorning of plaiting the hair, and of wearing of gold, or of putting on of apparel; But let it be the hidden man of the heart, in that which is not corruptible, even the ornament of a meek and quiet spirit, which is in the sight of God of great price. For after this manner in the old time the holy women also, who trusted in God, adorned themselves, being in subjection unto their own husbands: Even as Sara obeyed Abraham, calling him Lord: whose daughters ye are, as long as ye do well, and are not afraid with any amazement" (1 Peter 3:1, 3-6).

"Let no corrupt communication proceed out of your mouth, but that which is good to the use of edifying, that it may minister grace unto the hearers. And grieve not the holy Spirit of God, whereby ye are sealed unto the day of redemption. Let all bitterness, and wrath, and anger, and clamour, and evil speaking, be put away from you, with all malice: And be ye kind one to another, tenderhearted, forgiving one another, even as God for Christ's sake hath forgiven you" (Ephesians 4:29-32).

Wives are called to be a helpmeet, a crown, and a compliment to their husbands. Not a nag. When you choose to nag because "it works," then you are choosing to sin and say to God, "I know You said not to nag, but Your way didn't work, so I chose my way."

Ouch.

Choosing sin produces more sin.

Is being in sin and out of fellowship with God worth nagging your husband? Over what? The dishes? Vacuuming? Changing the light bulb? Cleaning the gutters?

I sure hope not.

The Root of Nagging: Selfishness and Entitlement. Which really boils down to pride.

"Only by pride cometh contention: but with the well advised is wisdom" (Proverbs 13:10).

"Pride goeth before destruction, and an haughty spirit before a fall" (Proverbs 16:18).

You're saying that what you want to happen is the essential thing that needs to be done, and it better be done right now. If not, you get angry and nag because your request isn't met when and how you want it to be, without regard to your husband's wants/needs. Just as you strongly want something done, he may equally not want to do it. Why is one more important than the other?

It is okay to *ask* him to do something. To point out the burnt-out light bulb with a kind, "Hey honey, the light above the sink is burnt out. Could you change it for me?" If it's not done in a few days, gently ask again. "I just want to remind you the light above the sink is out."

If he doesn't get it in another day or so, change the lightbulb. Him not changing it isn't a sin. Changing it yourself isn't the end of the world, either.

It is not okay to demand he change it right now, nor is it okay to yell at him to change it. If you can't be kind and respectful when you speak to your husband, don't speak.

You'll be better off praying while changing the lightbulb and skipping the arguments, hateful comments, and attitudes.

"Even a fool, when he holdeth his peace, is counted wise: and he that shutteth his lips is esteemed a man of understanding" (Proverbs 17:28).

The rule of treating others as you want to be treated isn't just for elementary school children. "Therefore all things whatsoever ye would that men should do to you, do ye even so to them: for this is the law and the prophets" (Matthew 7:12).

"Depart from evil, and do good; seek peace, and pursue it" (Psalm 34:14).

"A soft answer turneth away wrath: but grievous words stir up anger. The tongue of the wise useth knowledge aright: but the mouth of fools poureth out foolishness. The eyes of the Lord are in every place, beholding the evil and the good. A wholesome tongue is a tree of life: but perverseness therein is a breach in the spirit" (Proverbs 15:1-4).

"Every wise woman buildeth her house: but the foolish plucketh it down with her hands" (Proverbs 14:1).

"Through wisdom is an house builded; and by understanding it is established" (Proverbs 24:3).

Seek God at the sink and ask Him to help you be Christ-like, a servant, and encouragement in your home.

Day Twenty-Six
I've Lost Myself

Have you ever said or thought this? That you have lost yourself in being a wife and mother?
I do not want to downplay how you feel. Being a wife and mother can be challenging and overwhelming, especially in those early days of no sleep, temper tantrums, and potty training.

However, I want to help you. In love, I want to offer a new perspective and a realistic look at your flesh and feelings.

I recently took to Instagram to ask others how they felt about this statement. The responses were very similar. The responses included things like not having time for hobbies/personal interests, not being independent, missing careers, and time/trips with friends and family.

None of these things are wrong or sinful in and of themselves. They become sinful when they are your primary focus.

If you worked a lot before marriage/children, did you ever think, "I've lost myself in this job? I don't even know who I am anymore"? If not, why? It didn't bother you to give everything you had to a job and a boss who didn't love you; why is giving yourself to your family different?

Why can't you *find* yourself in this season? Why can't these responsibilities be fulfilling?

Maybe you did not lose yourself in becoming a wife and mother; instead, you found another part of yourself you never needed before.

Becoming a wife and mother forces you to become selfless. You have new responsibilities now that require you to care for others. Feeling like you have lost yourself because you are not focusing solely on your hobbies, goals, wants, and desires is an incorrect perspective. You must get past this, or you will become bitter toward those you love.

As a Christian, you are not to focus on yourself. Christ was not self-focused. Your focus should be on others. Romans 12:10 says to prefer one another. This is to put others before yourself.

I urge you to be honest with God about these feelings and pray for His help to shift your focus. Talk with your husband about these feelings and work to make time for a hobby, date night, working out, etc., but stay flexible. Remember, these activities are fine, but they are not the priority. If you decide that every Monday night from 8-9 P.M., you can watch television in silence, go to the gym, read, take a bubble bath, etc., but then a child is sick, your husband is sick, you have company, or your husband works late, do not get bitter or angry over this. Pray against those feelings and pick back up next week.

Part of these feelings are from your flesh, but they are also from the world. Society puts no value on being a wife and mother. The world says marriage isn't valuable and mothers are replaceable. Culture encourages you to live together and have children together, but to put those children in daycare and school as soon as possible.

You must look to the Word of God for your value. Children are gifts from the Lord, and God has handpicked you to raise those children. That was not an accident or mistake. Your husband and marriage are also gifts from the Lord. You and your husband have become one flesh. Marriage requires giving up the independence you had as a single person.

God values your work and influence in the home. A godly wife and mother who joyfully serves her family will make an impact for eternity. It is easy to feel that earning a paycheck and working for the next promotion are the only worthy goals. If God has called you to work outside the home, that's great, but He does not ever want you to give more to your job than your family.

Working is hard. Staying home is hard. Both must be done as unto the Lord and only as He leads. If He has called you to stay home, please do, and rely on Him to do it well. Refrain from spending your days thinking the grass is greener in the next pasture. It's not.

If you feel unfulfilled as a wife and mother, that's okay because these are not meant to fulfill you. Your hobbies will not fulfill you. Your job will not fulfill you. Christ alone fulfills you. You must look to Him. He wants you to have joy in your day, but you will not have this apart from Him.

There will be hard days, but you must learn to take those challenging days to the Saviour. Do not let them make you bitter or second-guess His calling on your life.

I am going to leave you with Scripture. Take the time to look these up, write them down, and pray them back to the Lord.

Isaiah 58:11
Psalm 90:14
Proverbs 31
Hebrews 12:2
Psalm 107:9
Matthew 5:1-12
Psalm 127:3
Matthew 19:6
Proverbs 14:1
Proverbs 21:9 and verse 19
Proverbs 27:15
Philippians 4:11
Hebrews 13:5
1 Timothy 6:6
Proverbs 14:30

There will be trials. There will be days when you make bedtime an hour early because you need a break. Using a Mother's Day Out program or babysitter is okay! It is essential to have quality alone time with your husband. It is not sinful to have desires and hobbies. But your priorities must stay in the correct order: God, husband, children, and then everything else. Do not let selfishness or discontentment keep you from being a godly wife and mom.

I do not want to leave you feeling guilty or judged. That is not my heart or my intent. I know the joy of being a wife and mother. I also know the struggle of the "what-ifs." I know the financial change of being a one-income household. I know the days of being home all day without adult conversation. I know these feelings are real and natural. But you have to take them to the Lord. Go to the Lord with these feelings, just as you take thoughts and feelings of not liking someone or being worried about something to the Lord.

It has been nine years since I started staying home and homeschooling. We made this change after I spent two years in college. I had the what-ifs and guilt of not using my EMT certification and not finishing my RN degree. I watched my friends graduate college and get good jobs. I have been there. I know the days spent at home are long. But I also know the years are short. Do not wish them away.

I also know how Satan attacks the thoughts of a wife to cause discontentment, division, and disaster. Stay vigilant.

I will not pretend to understand your challenges or God's will for you. But I do know He wants you to trust Him, to serve joyfully in your home, to point your children to Him, and to be content.

He may be using this season to grow you.

Seek God at the sink. Whether crying real tears or just pouring your heart out through prayer. Take all of your struggles and what-ifs to Him.

Day Twenty-Seven
The Titus 2 Woman: Part 1

There is no shortage of articles, blogs, and memes depicting Biblical womanhood. What do most of them have in common? They almost always use the Proverbs 31 woman. That passage has a wealth of knowledge, and you should know what the Bible says about her. But what about the Titus 2 woman?

Titus 2:3-5 says, "The aged women likewise, that they be in behaviour as becometh holiness, not false accusers, not given to much wine, teachers of good things; That they may teach the young women to be sober, to love their husbands, to love their children, To be discreet, chaste, keepers at home, good, obedient to their own husbands, that the word of God be not blasphemed."

There are several attainable and admirable qualities here. Attainability is very important. You must remember that these qualities come over time. You will not wake up one day at 65 years old and happen to be a godly woman. This starts with the choices you make now.

One way to do this is by living in the light of eternity. Heaven will be here sooner than you think. The next generation will not be babies long. Your lifestyle, your testimony, matters today.

No doubt the Titus 2 woman is lovable and honorable. What does this passage teach exactly?

1. The aged woman is to be living a holy life. A life of righteousness that is

pleasing to the Lord. She has a godly testimony. There isn't anything questionable in her life, including her attitude. She remembers that things aren't about her. They're about the Lord; she seeks to honor and glorify Him. That others look at her and see Jesus.

2. Not a false accuser. She avoids gossip and scandal.
3. Not given to much wine. She is not controlled by alcohol. Sober is also being vigilant.
4. Teachers of good things. She uses the Bible as her guide and teaches the younger women. She has quite a list of things to model and teach them. All of these qualities that the younger women should learn are for one purpose: that the word of God be not blasphemed.

So, what is it that she needs to teach?

Verse 4: "That they may teach the young women to be sober, to love their husbands, to love their children," The first thing to note is not about what she is to be teaching, but rather the attitude of the younger woman. You must be teachable. You will not be teachable if you aren't willing to admit that you do not know everything.

When you are in church, and the Sunday school teacher or the pastor says to open to Proverbs 31, Ephesians 5, or Colossians 3, what is your attitude? If an aged woman tries to offer advice and encouragement, give her your full attention.

What she is to teach:

    1. To be sober. Remember the aged woman's example of not being controlled by wine? Soberness is something the younger woman desperately needs to learn. Especially in today's society. How often are you casually drinking with friends, at dinner, lunch, and other opportunity? You must realize that you do not *need* that in your life. Again, to be vigilant also. Do not accept all doctrines that are taught. False doctrines are taught as being Biblical, including progressive Christianity. Satan has a counterfeit for everything. His lies sound good and even close to the truth; this is why you must know the Bible. Being sober also pertains to moderation in all things. Too much eating, shopping, television, social media, etc., cause you not to be vigilant.

Why is this a big deal? Because you have an enemy that is constantly seeking to destroy you. Never lose sight of what God is doing in your life, but never forget the reality of Satan and spiritual warfare (1 Peter 5:8).

    2. To love their husbands. This is the only place in Scripture where women are told

to love their husbands and need to be *taught* how to do it.

Do you find this strange? In your own nature, you love. That's just how God made women. In other verses, God tells the wife to submit and the husband to love. The Hebrew language is more complex than the English language, and I am not a Hebrew scholar. However, the 'love' used here is different from the same word in other places. The English language only has one word, while the Hebrew has multiple. This is not 'agape' love; it is 'phileo' love, referring to affection, emotion, fondness, and brotherly love.

Women know how to deeply, unconditionally love. But that doesn't always equate to a fundamental friendship-type love towards their husbands. This is something that must be learned. Phileo love is basic kindness and compassion. To actually *like* your husband and care for him.

This order also shows that your husband comes before your children. If your husband and marriage are not a priority, things will be out of balance, and your marriage will suffer. Disorder opens many opportunities for Satan to enter your home and marriage.

3. To love their children. The same word of love is used here. You are to be their parent, not their friend, but this doesn't mean you are an unemotional drill sergeant. That's not what God wants. You should be showing your children affection and kindness. You should like

them and want to have a relationship with them.

4. To be discreet. To be sensible, mature, not silly. To be careful and circumspect, not causing offense. This does not mean to be silent and never speak the truth for fear of offending. Verse 3 said to be teachers of good things. Just know that there are times to be serious and times to be lighthearted.

5. Chaste. Simple, not dressed provocatively, as to have sexual intentions, not having extramarital sexual affairs. You are not to draw the attention or entertain the advances of men you are not married to.

6. Keepers at home. You are to work and be busy in your home. The home is the wife's first priority. You are also to guard your home and the things that come into it.

7. Good. To be kind. In word and deed. Proverbs 31:26

8. Obedient to their own husbands. This is clear. See also Ephesians 5:22, 5:24, and Colossians 3:18. God has given the husband the authority of being the head of the home, and wives are to submit to that authority.

The result of these commands is that the word of God does not get blasphemed. Do not allow the word of

God to be spoken evilly of or disregarded in your home. You must make it a priority in your life and live by example. Teach and train your kids to have devotions, pray, and live according to the Bible. Speak with your husband about not allowing evil shows, movies, and music into the home. Everyone has a different stance here, and that's okay. Some things to begin watching for are things that mock Dad as the authority, things that take God's name in vain, and sexual content.

Live by these commands in public and private. Let this be your true testimony that honors God's Word and shows others His Word works.

All women need a variety of friends. If you are a young woman, there are some specific ladies you should have in your circle. Widows, seasoned saints, women your age and in the same stage of life, and women in different stages of life regardless of age. You always have something to learn from each of them.

Read your Bible, fellowship with those women, and read good biblical books and blogs to help you continue to grow. Do not stop trying to improve yourself and your relationship with the Lord and your family. You cannot teach these truths to others if you do not live them out.

Aged women, you are still needed. Don't stop teaching the younger wives. Your wisdom, knowledge, and experience are all precious. God is not finished with you yet.

Seek God at the sink and ask Him to help you be a woman willing to learn and grow so you can teach others.

Day Twenty-Eight
The Titus 2 Woman: Part 2

Yesterday's reading covered verses three through five. Today will cover verses seven through fifteen.

I truly love God's Word and how He teaches us so much in just a few verses. I believe verse 7 begins instructing all Christians, not just men or women, as we have experienced in previous verses.

The Bible says: "In all things shewing thyself a pattern of good works: in doctrine shewing uncorruptness, gravity, sincerity, Sound speech, that cannot be condemned; that he that is of the contrary part may be ashamed, having no evil thing to say of you. Exhort servants to be obedient unto their own masters, and to please them well in all things; not answering again; Not purloining, but shewing all good fidelity; that they may adorn the doctrine of God our Saviour in all things. For the grace of God that bringeth salvation hath appeared to all men, Teaching us that, denying ungodliness and worldly lusts, we should live soberly, righteously, and godly, in this present world; Looking for that blessed hope, and the glorious appearing of the great God and our Saviour Jesus Christ; Who gave himself for us, that he might redeem us from all iniquity, and purify unto himself a peculiar people, zealous of good works. These things speak, and exhort, and rebuke with all authority. Let no man despise thee" (Titus 2:7-15).

Verse 7: In all things. You are to have a pattern of good works in every area of your life. This is part of daily life; it's just who you are. Doing something good or godly now and then does not fit this description.

What are the good works you should be doing? Verse 7 explains that in doctrine (your beliefs and teachings), you are to show uncorruptness. This is a pure belief that aligns with Scripture. God has a lot to say about false teachers throughout His Word. Always check to be sure you are not in that camp. Stick with Scripture as it is written. You do not need a new interpretation or another modern explanation. God has given it just as He wants you to have it.

You are to show gravity in your teachings. This is to be serious and thoughtful, keeping it a matter of importance. Do not get to a place where the Word of God is not a priority to you.

You are to show sincerity in your teachings. This is teaching with honesty of mind and freedom from hypocrisy. Teach what Scripture says even if others may disagree, but do not change your beliefs of Scripture because someone disagrees with you.

Teach with sound speech that cannot be condemned. When you give the truth, the Holy Spirit does the rest to show the hearers that it is truth. He is the one who brings comfort and conviction. But you must give the truth in love so the hearer will receive it. Speaking in a condemning, hateful, forceful way is not speech that can't be condemned. Remember that your speech is to always be seasoned with salt and grace, acceptable unto God. When you speak like this, those who are contrary, opposing God, are convicted by the Holy Spirit, convinced of the truth, and have nothing negative to say of you. As I said in the beginning, some of these are hard to teach and even harder to receive, but I am trying to share these truths from a place of love and kindness.

Verses 9-10 deal with the servant/master relationship. You can apply this to your job as well. Your work attitude should be one of seeking to do your job thoroughly and honestly. Having a good testimony at work honors the Lord.

Verse 11 is interesting. "For the grace of God that bringeth salvation hath appeared to all men," Everyone has experienced the grace of God. It is by God's grace you are saved through faith. God's grace not only saves, but as you see in verse 12, it teaches what to leave, how to live, and what to look for.

First, He says to deny ungodliness. This is anything that is in opposition to God. Sin, ungodly living, things that reject or disobey God. Next, He instructs you to deny worldly lusts- the pleasure or desire in sinful behaviors. This desire is part of your flesh and fallen nature. You will battle this, but God wants you to grow spiritually and learn to desire the things of God. Psalm 1:2 says, "But his delight is in the law of the LORD; and in his law doth he meditate day and night." This is speaking of the one who chooses to walk with God. You will develop godly desires if you allow God to work in your heart.

Next, He says to live soberly. This is not just living free from being intoxicated with drugs and alcohol. It is also living seriously, thoughtfully, and not in extreme qualities of emotion. This command is also given in verses 2-4 and 6 of this chapter. But God does not stop there. He also addresses this in 1 Peter 5:8, 1 Thessalonians 5:6, and 1 Timothy 3:11. God is very serious about living soberly, acknowledging spiritual truths.

This is the idea of paying attention or being vigilant. He is not saying that you can never joke, relax, and have a good time, but that you are to be filled (or controlled by) the Holy Spirit. This is how you begin to live out this verse. (See also Acts 13:52 and Ephesians 5:18).

Secondly, God says you are to live righteously. This is to be free from guilt or sin, to be morally right. You are never going to be perfect, but you are to be seeking to live as God wants you to, and when you sin, confess it to the Lord and ask for His help to not fall into that sin again.

Next, you are to live godly. This is living a life that reflects God to others. This is the opposite of the above definition of ungodliness and worldly lusts.

The last phrase is "in this present world." God wants you to live this way right now. Amid the sin and chaos around you, you can live a godly life and raise godly children. God did not put you here, allow you to live in this space of time, for you to fail. He wants you to live godly right now, with His help. Your lifestyle and faithfulness to God may just be the thing that brings someone else to Jesus.

God's grace should be producing godliness in you, not worldliness. His grace is a gift and should never be used as permission to sin.

Verse 13 says, "Looking for that blessed hope," this is to live in the joyful assurance that Jesus will return. Looking is a present tense verb. It is what you are to be actively doing right now. Living in hope and expectancy that Jesus will come back. First Thessalonians 4 is all about the return of the Lord and how that is to be a comfort for Christians. His return is not the end of your life but the beginning of your life in Heaven with God for all eternity. Nothing is better than that! Because of this truth, you should share God's Word daily so that others may know and come to salvation before it is too late.

Verse 14 shows what Christ has done in the life of every Christian. His blood and finished work at the Cross have set you free, redeemed, and set you apart. You should be different from the lost people around you, different from a sinful society.

You have been set on fire. Remember when you first got saved and were so on fire for Jesus? Every person you met soon learned you had been saved. Where has that zeal gone? It's time to stop suppressing what God is doing and has done for you and start telling others again.

Verse 15 is a clear command to speak these things, encourage others, rebuke when necessary in the authority of Scripture, and let no one condescend or speak badly of you, and it be true. Live soberly, righteously, and godly in this present world through the help and leading of the Holy Spirit.

Remember the difference this will make in your life and home if you trust God and be a Titus 2 woman.

Seek God at the sink, and ask Him to guide you to live according to Scripture and apart from this present world.

Day Twenty-Nine
Worship the Right Table

I love reminders to return to the dinner table. It is a place of physical nourishment, fellowship, laughter, and memories. Families need this time of intentional connection. Too many families live separate lives, occasionally glancing at one another from behind our screens. This is not how God intended your home to be.

You need to eat meals together, spend time together, have a conversation and quality time. I am not saying to abandon the dinner table, family time, or game night. However, you're not failing as a mother/wife/family if you eat on the couch watching a movie together.

As a parent, you are to teach and train your children. You are the example they will model their lives by. You are also to bring them up in the nurture and admonition of the Lord. Part of being that example is showing healthy boundaries with technology, how to communicate with others, and that all they do should honor the Lord. It is your responsibility to be involved in their lives. Know what is happening at school, if they're struggling with homework, and who they are talking with.

It is easy to say, "I don't understand technology. There's a new app out every day." New apps are coming out daily, but that doesn't mean you or your child must be on them.

I spent five and a half months working with teenage girls in a Christian girls' home. The things I learned about the internet from them were astounding! Some websites practically do homework for them, group chats where they share answers, and the parents and teachers never had a clue! The work was completed, the kids had decent grades, and that's all that mattered.

It's time to get involved in your kids' lives. You must be available to them if you want to hear from them.

It's time to stop focusing solely on being around the dinner table and get them around God's table. They need to be taught and encouraged biblically. They need to know how to walk with God and to cast their cares upon Him. They will not figure this out on their own. They will not live godly lives, have convictions, or even get to Heaven when this life is over by accident!

Psalm 23:5-6 offers very comforting words: "Thou preparest a table before me in the presence of mine enemies: thou anointest my head with oil; my cup runneth over. Surely goodness and mercy shall follow me all the days of my life: and I will dwell in the house of the LORD for ever." This is both a praise and a promise. God wants you to come and dine with Him at His table.

How do you get there? Psalm 23:1 gives that answer: "The LORD is my shepherd; I shall not want." You will not have access to His table if He is not your Shepherd.

Christ must be a part of your daily life. That is how your children will come to know Him.
Stop worshiping the dining room table and begin worshiping around His table together. Bring your children to Jesus.

Seek God at the sink and ask Him to guide you as you become involved in your children's lives and daily lead them to Jesus.

Day Thirty
The Loud and Stubborn Woman

Proverbs 7:11 says, "She is loud and stubborn; her feet abide not in her house:"

This verse begins to describe a harlot. We could get into many lessons with this, but I want to focus on this phrase.

It describes many women today, doesn't it? In today's culture, this is not just the harlot. The world tells women to be loud and stubborn, that these characteristics are something to be proud of. However, the truth is these are not attributes of a godly woman.

The woman in Proverbs 7 used her loud words to bring others to sin. This is the power of your influence and words! Choose to be a woman who uses her words for good.

Proverbs 31:26 says, "She openeth her mouth with wisdom; and in her tongue is the law of kindness." Godly speech is wise and kind and will not cause others to sin.

First Timothy 5:13 says, "And withal they learn to be idle, wandering from house to house; and not only idle, but tattlers also and busybodies, speaking things which they ought not." When not staying in your own business, you are idle (wasting time and energy) and gossiping. This is not being a godly woman or having godly speech.

Titus 2:3-5 commands, "The aged women likewise, that they be in behaviour as becometh holiness, not false accusers, not given to much wine, teachers of good things; Thay they may teach the young women to be sober, to love their husbands, to love their children, To be discreet, chaste, keepers at home, good, obedient to their own husbands, that the word of God be not blasphemed."

You are called to be a godly woman who lives a holy life, teaching younger women to live godly, while keeping a humble heart so you may continue to learn from other godly women. This is not a life that is loud and stubborn.

First Peter 3:1-4 says, "Likewise, ye wives, be in subjection to your own husbands; that, if any obey not the word, they also may without the word be won by the conversation of the wives; While they behold your chaste conversation coupled with fear. Whose adorning let it not be that outward adorning of plaiting the hair, and of wearing of gold, or of putting on of apparel; But let it be that hidden man of the heart. In that which is not corruptible, even the ornament of a meek and quiet spirit, which is in the sight of God of great price."

Loud and stubborn women are not submissive; they draw attention to themselves, their lifestyles are not chaste, and they do not have a meek and quiet spirit.

Additionally, being stubborn is not the same as standing your ground and not moving from your convictions.

Colossians 2:7 says, "Rooted and built up in him, and stablished in the faith, as ye have been taught, abounding therein with thanksgiving."

God wants you to be firm in His Word and your faith. But this does not negate having a godly attitude while standing firm. This is not being stubborn and unwilling to learn and submit to God's Word.

Seek God at the sink. Pray to be a godly woman who draws others to Christ rather than yourself, have a meek and quiet spirit, and speak with wisdom and kindness.

Day Thirty-One
The Vineyard of Your Life

"I went by the field of the slothful, and by the vineyard of the man void of understanding; And, lo, it was all grown over with thorns, and nettles had covered the face thereof, and the stone wall thereof was broken down. Then I saw, and considered it well: I looked upon it, and received instruction. Yet a little sleep, a little slumber, a little folding of the hands to sleep: So shall thy poverty come as one that travelleth; and thy want as an armed man" (Proverbs 24:30-34).

Do you see the imagery here?

Imagine walking down a dirt road with an overgrown field to your left. You see parts of a broken-down stone wall overtaken with thorns, nettles, and weeds. This overgrown mess stretches all through the rest of the field.

What used to be here? What happened to this place?

A little sleep, a little slumber, a little folding of the hands to sleep.

Just a little.

A little procrastination. A little laziness.

A little is all it takes to end up with a big mess.

These thorns, nettles, and weeds got into this vineyard because neglect allowed them to. A little time pulling weeds was too much for the vineyard's keeper. A little weed seemed insignificant.

Until it wasn't.

The thorns and nettles have caused more than just a cosmetic problem. Their roots go much deeper than that. The roots have worked through the soil, under the wall, through its cracks, and into the root system of the fruit the vineyard was to produce. Everything has been touched and overtaken by them.

A small compromise led to a big problem.

A small choice led to significant consequences.

A once strong and sturdy wall is now broken down and crumbling.

What have you allowed into the soil of your heart?

What small weed did you allow to grow?

What has taken root in your life?

What has caused your once solid and steady convictions to crumble?

The things of this world get into the soil of your life, and when left to grow, they will cause problems. Broken-down walls leave you susceptible to the enemy and his attacks. Before long, you and others look at this overgrown space and wonder what happened. You wonder how you got here. What was once a sturdy wall is now a pile of rubble. What was once a growing and thriving vineyard is now in shambles, totally unproductive.

Is this your life?

Can you look to the past and see when you walked closely with God? When missing church wasn't an option? When serving Him wasn't a burden? When telling others about Him wasn't a fleeting thought?

If that's you, look at the present state of your vineyard.

What happened?

Pride?

Bitterness?

Laziness?

Hurt?

Busyness?

Whatever has crept into the vineyard, it's time to get it out.

It is time to start the cleanup process.

It is time to rebuild the wall.

It is time to begin sowing godly seeds again.

Get back to tending the vineyard.

"Looking diligently lest any man fail of the grace of God; lest any root of bitterness springing up trouble you, and thereby many be defiled;" (Hebrews 12:15).

"That he would grant you, according to the riches of his glory, to be strengthened with might by his Spirit in the inner man; That Christ may dwell in your hearts by faith; that ye, being rooted and grounded in love, May be able to comprehend with all saints what is the breadth, and length, and depth, and height; And to know the love of Christ, which passeth knowledge, that ye might be filled with all the fulness of God" (Ephesians 3:16-19).

On our final day together, seek God at the sink.

Ask Him to help you make or keep your life one that honors Him, serves, influences, and brings others to Him.

Thank you for taking the time to read this devotional. I pray it has helped and challenged you to grow spiritually and take God at His Word. God loves you, wants to help you, and wants you to use His Word as your guide.

Keep seeking Him at the sink, and teach your children and others to do the same.

Made in United States
North Haven, CT
14 June 2024

53646953R00065